ENTER

This is number 168
of a limited edition
of 500 copies

Laurence Whistler

Other books by Laurence Whistler

ON HIS ENGRAVINGS

The Engraved Glass of Laurence Whistler (1952)
Engraved Glass 1952–1958 (1959)
Pictures on Glass (1972)
The Image on the Glass (1975)
Scenes and Signs on Glass (1985)

PROSE

The English Festival (1947)
The Initials in the Heart (1964, re-issued 1987)

POETRY

The World's Room: Collected Poems (1949)
The View from This Window (1956)
Audible Silence (1961)
To Celebrate Her Living (1967)

ON REX WHISTLER

Rex Whistler, His Life and His Drawings (1948)
The Work of Rex Whistler (with Ronald Fuller) (1969)
¡OHO! (1947) *AHA* (1978) (verses to Rex Whistler's Reversible Faces)
The Laughter and the Urn: The Life of Rex Whistler (1985 and 1986)

ON ARCHITECTURE

Sir John Vanbrugh, Architect and Dramatist (1938)
The Imagination of Vanbrugh and His Fellow Artists (1954)

ENTER

Laurence Whistler

with an afterword by
Christopher Booker

WEIDENFELD AND NICOLSON
LONDON

The five pictures are of glasses engraved by the poet. Two are goblets, and three are from a window in the parish church of Curry Rivel in Somerset.

This collection of poems
first published in Great Britain by
George Weidenfeld & Nicolson Limited
91 Clapham High Street
London SW4 7TA

ISBN 0 297 79245 8

Printed in Great Britain by
Butler & Tanner Ltd, Frome and London

For

CAROL

in bright evening

Contents

OTHER POEMS

WHO LIVE IN UNITY

I

And there, quite silently and like a toy
Returning to a hand, the train. And then
Out of that desert of her being away
She issued with the strangeness of some flower,
Strange even to him who pictured it so clearly,
So feverishly clearly, the one flower.

He wore her like a flower. And every time
Her strangeness, when he pinned it to his heart,
Wilted and died, another quickly seemed
To glow, tremble and harden out of the air itself,
That heady and high ether of excitement
In which the miracle might always bud.

But in between the miracles were gaps
When she was only green, only green leaves
That twisted from a bed, and drowned a house,
And lulled that house with murmurs of light hearts.
Lost in those glades—laughter from room to room—
He followed music to the urn of silence
Into which music plunges, and glides on.
Then they seemed best of all, the gaps of green,
The flowerless boughs of all her tendernesses.

II

Now, surely, love is easy to construe—
Now, surely, the queer grammar is resolved,
The mood imperative, the meaning stark,
Now, while between the subtle-shaded lamps
She leans, and in her breathless mirror stares,
Willing its troubled chaos to receive
Absolute beauty, like a universe;
Or adds lash after lash, new points to a dark star.

Those final stars, that long carved scroll of hair,
The great red buckle diminishing the waist,
Those entwined legs that sharpen into heels,
And the young mouth
(Bracketted in faint lines for passion's use)
Whose upper lip she'll form in a dark petal,
Then print the other from it and compose
The total rose—
Now surely love is finite in that rose!

But no, inside her, though unreachable,
Still threaded through her like a kind of fuse,
Though finer than a hair,
Is something vastly more significant
Yet weaker than the single-minded rose,
Weaker with self-awareness, flawed with doubt.
See where it humbly now, and soberly,
Waits in the soft excitement of the lamps
To judge that mirrored face, as any gilder
Judges gilding, pleased, but critical,
And wholly unimpressed!

So hangs her beauty on that thread, the soul.
But he who watches, with the watchful room,
His provocation winked from bottles and
Secretive in a dozen little jars,
Cannot remember. She to him is all
Resolved into the flawless certainty
And simple invitation of a rose.
But rather is she now to him a cliff
From which a cataract with smiling lip
Leans, framing the hard challenge, Dare to jump!
For she is danger. O she is the stranger.
Rather she is the foreigner, with all
The fascinating difference, all the charm
Of a strange country somewhere under foot,
The marvellous antipodes of sex.

Then all at once it will flow back in him
Like a forgotten fragrance. He'll remember
Who she is, half sad that to remember
Is also to forget; for she will be
No longer strange. It will be only curious
To know she was ever strange, whose body moves
On the same gradual tide of breath toward
The dunes of sleep, with the same drift as his.
In brief removing fire
Passion will have fallen from her like a garment
Whispering to her heels. And so, at last,
She will be naked for him, and not strange,
But loved entirely, all her weakness known.
Then it may seem to him as if he merely
Had rediscovered an old, intimate friend,
Yet someone nearer, less defined than friend;
Almost his other face, almost himself.

Then all the colours will run out and blur
The picturebook of selves. And then there will be
neither
He and she, nor even one and one,
But, vaguely, one.
Enormity of London,
The rumour of that murmur, will reduce
Time to a trickle. The electric fire
Will give the ceiling one unearthly smile
Like an arrested sunset. They will sleep.

III

All night her dreams roared in her ears
Like swimming under water. So she swam,
Wide-eyed among the inconsistences,
Until some rock of vague disquietude
Loomed at her fingers; and she clutched at it,
Hauled herself up into the other world,
Heavy beneath a slipping cape of sleep,
And lay there, languid, conscious only of warmth,
In the bed's secret summer, a dark sunlight.
Then the curtain moved.

At once, a mouse
Rattled like a little marble across the ceiling,
As if it waited only for that cue.
This complicated darkness streaming through time
In a fixed order, this logical cataract,
Was her own world, her present—present as something
given,
As unique gift. Slowly her hand went out

And touched him, found him actual—the dull shoulder
Bent to the job of sleeping. It was true.
Gravely assured, she turned from him, let go,
Cast backward, loosened, slid away.

A white arm circled.
                                        Then again the sea's
Indistinct conversation filled her ears.

IV

To be presented with a day—
As if one should discover on the quilt
This overwhelming present, a white day,
Unwritten, just created, still a blank,
Quickly to be removed, and then given back
Bound up in some relentless manuscript.
To have the illuminating of this day. To be
There at the extension of eternity,
Time flattened out like vellum in the hands
Or equally a scribbling pad; and know
That even a doodle in the margin may reveal
Descent from Michelangelo.

   To know the tree the lightning cracks
   That gives the bough to the swung axe
   That piles the cart that feeds the flame
   That wills its ashes to the same
   Dark need of earth that yet must be
   Used and delivered of a tree—
         This is the house that God built.

To feel around the candlestick
That holds the match that gives the wick
A listening-for-someone eye
That looks on nightmares quietly—
For all re-entries into night,
For meditation in sweet light,
This is the house.

To know the stream that fills the pool
That fills the jug that fills the bowl
That fills the cupped and thoughtful palms
With water gentle as an alms—
The house of the good life must be
Even so in all simplicity.
This is.

Simplicity is a rare virtue. They learnt
From nearness to the ancient elements
The sanctity of matter. The ambitious flame,
The cloud-kind water, the inventive earth,
And the white scent of an unscented air
Included them in holy sequences,
And had such borrowed splendour they believed
A sun was active behind everything,
And everything was luminous, and thin.
Thus matter, ghostly as cathedral glass,
Showed them her colours as they moved together,
Charmed by the colours, conscious of the sun.

V

Sometimes when strolling the reflective hills
Alone, or in the street, concealed in idiot clamour,
Perfectly happy, private, and obscure,
He would stop short to question such content—
Have I forgotten? Is it a pretence?
Does it mean anything?—She seemed no more
A dazzle like the horizontal sun,
Love's vanishing-point or point of origin,
But rather the inert illuminated,
The circling traffic or encircling hills:
To have become the stuff of otherness
And been dissolved in things. He could not see
Her image. It was everywhere he looked,
Or nowhere. He could only breathe it in.

Sometimes when night was pastoral, and they
Were tuned to its vibrato candlelight
As to a low recorder—using words,
Yet hardly noticing the words, so rapt
In the fine harmonies mere thinking made,
Mere thought with thought, like fingered bell with
bell,
Blooming and waning, audible tenderness—
A curious notion came. All this exists
In one mind only. Whose? Am I asleep?—
Or am I mad, and talking to myself?

If she became a stranger, he was saved.

VI

Like the revolving towers of that storm,
Their quarrel had been piling up for hours
Before it happened. They kept moving round,
Contriving to be busy, all the time
Held to each other by a sultry warmth,
Drawn to each other by love, angrily.
So they arrived at speaking: a new speech,
Not fugal and suggestive, all loose ends,
But measured, dangerously logical.
At that they heard the quick loud drops thumb all the panes.

Now each knew well the fight was lower down
Than words, raged on the dark floor underneath
Where words are impotent. There, elementals,
Bits of themselves, agents without a name—
Call them perhaps Ambition, Jealousy,
Or Pride—stormed to and fro, slamming the doors.
Words were a game, a game with some connection
With what went on below-stairs. Thus, until
That hubbub spent itself, the game went on,
For heat can mumble round a sky into next month.

Q to K 4. That move was justly made.
That was well put. So. And I counter—so.
Check. Countercheck! Each in exasperation
Heard his impeachments whistled back again,
Like parley with a parrot, recognised
All his spoilt grudges in the other's play.
By now the deckle edge of darkness held
Suppressed amusement, in a strip of light.
What sort of game is this? Where are the rules?

'Narrow'. 'Disloyal'. 'Ruthless'. Who is accusing
whom?

So it was over, without artistry,
With no decisions reached, and neither party
Satisfied, and nothing proved at all.
Yet, instinct knew it over. *For a time*
The indecisions of the rain wore on
In anticlimax. For a time the word
They both were wishing now had not been said,
The word too cutting, or the word too true,
Kept bringing footsteps to the floor beneath,
Which, padding to and fro, ached like a healing bruise.

Afterwards they discovered how the hills,
Playing grandmother's steps, had stolen up
Quite close about them smiling. In the middle,
A consequential train from a Victorian plate
Put up into the round, delighted air
Five balls of steam

VII

Once in a hundred lives—
For days are complete lives, and every day
Out of chaotic shadow they were born
Into each other, a calm universe,
And every night, welcoming chaos, died—
Once in a hundred loves,
Love failed, or wishing failed.
Their wishes, like joined hands,
That should have lifted up

To faint excited horns and triangles
One hour, or moment, like a cup to Joy
Itself, the revealed eye in everything,
Doubted. They heard it drop.
They who had heard no music heard it stop.

And they were strangely disinherited.
Cut off, not from their bodies, which could move,
They found, as hitherto; could eat and drink;
And presently, they even knew, would love;
But from all else, from literally all else.
A sun went in, and it was life grew cold
And grey, and slightly smaller than before.
And they lived on. And in between them and
Far off each numbly insulated act
There was a pane of nothing.
And each felt nothing; and was shut in nothing.

O quickly, wishes, open those clenched hands.
Only believe in touching, you will touch.
Touch—and the music will be there already
As if, but far away, some door had opened.
And they will see joy distantly, like sunlight
Learning a hill, and not yet felt—and then
Silently lavish, white and everywhere.
It will be rammed like meaning into matter
So as to enlarge and slightly loosen it.
Joy such as Adam woke to. Joy in this and that.
Joy in a cloud, a paper-weight, a chair.

VIII

A quaver glance is not indicative.
You can exchange them safely in the street,
Eye to eye linked, too brief a link for thought.
But hold it for one beat and see
How all your meaning has gushed out along
A dangerously overloaded wire!

One night when she came in,
Calm from the clear approval of her mirror
And conscious of her beauty like a scent,
Came softly in and he looked up at her,
The pressure of that glance
Became a fingertip laid secretly
Against her finger, instantly revealing
A whole immense design; and beckoning.
She gave no hint of recognition:
Moved on, touching the hair against her cheek:
Took something from the mantelpiece: observed it
With grave and heedless profile. Yet he knew
By those held lashes, by that faintly pouting,
Faintly still resisting mouth, he knew
She followed, she responded.

She would respond—no shepherd's champion Nell
Raced to so faint a whistle, nor violin
Answered so tentative a bow.

Things held their breath all round the room
To see them begin building their mad Folly
Of pleasure, as if building up with cards
A great and glitteringly fragile tower.

One falter here, one wish unshareable,
If he were not all ardour, and if she
Were not, to him, entirely beautiful—
The cards would stagger at a clumsy hand!
Things held their breath all round the room,
Tried to efface their unimportant shapes,
Even the clock ticked without emphasis,
And time grew humble.

But he was nothing but the contemplation
Of what she had become—a burning-glass,
All the wide sunlight of his happiness
Brought to one point of eating flame. And she,
She was entirely beautiful, like Venus
Waxing in glamour as the face of day
Effaced itself.

IX

To rise with groans: to explore curtained rooms,
Stuffy with shadows and small-talk of clocks.
To cross a field, and gather up again,
From habit, the untidy edge of self
With all its fears and wishes fraying out.
To bring this to the table then, resolving
On a new start. Yet, having reached the place,
Firstly to thank. For in that austere room
Where the stone smells of remote gratitude,
All joy is lovely, and all else observed,
And nothing's private, or beneath regard.

No secrets are hid

Though how to thank for that which in itself
Includes your thankfulness? For the first gift
So all-embracing it's impossible
To see? How to accept immortal life
As if it were no more than painted egg
Adorned with an initial—to receive
Such manna into hands not satisfied
Or ignorant, but hungrily aware?
By symbols only. For the soul is only
Nourished in ghostly parallel to symbols.
Lucid as kneeling, meek as candlelight.

Take, eat

Two candles only for the festival
Of all rekindled?
And one great window troubled with the dawn
As with too high an honour, showing
Part of an ash tree through ennobled panes:
The one dark bough of candelabrum buds,
And all those wicks on fire.
They waited, silent in the interval
Between two movements; say, between two lives.
Day now was cheapening the candles. Time was still
Plodding with numb footfalls in the tower.
But for one moment there had been a glimpse
Of the design, the meaning. Gone—and yet
Not utterly—still floating luminous
Just behind matter, just beyond range of mind:
To fascinate the corners of the eye.

And remain with you always

The Haunting

As we lay thinking side by side,
One afternoon years back,
And read the ceiling for pure joy,
And scanned it crack by crack,

Or wrote joy out in secret there
Round every cranny and blotch—
It seemed to me a shadow-man
Hung in the door to watch.

Familiar was he, like myself,
No stranger to our home,
Who, pausing for some faint salute,
Strolled out into the room.

Oddly detached, immune from fear,
I followed where he came,
Thinking, in his 'time', palpably
This room is much the same.

Moving and peering by the wall,
So narrowly he looks,
I vow his plates and pictures hang
From the same nails and hooks;

So knowingly he stands to con
The ceiling's faded maps,
He must find news of treasure there—
Such as we note, perhaps.

And then he shifted, vague as dust,
And bowed a sketchy head
Hopelessly transparent down
At your side of the bed,

And at the pillow stared, like one
Whom no denial cures,
As though with all his will to burn
Through from his time to yours.

Just then his window must have caught
The sun. (A cloud dimmed ours.)
I saw his face glow faintly on
Your dressing-table flowers.

Though middle-age had plumped the jowl,
Confirming crease and line,
I could not doubt whose looks they were.
Mine.

No Answer

In the slow lapse of unrecorded afternoon,
When nothing seems to change but history itself
Unfolding at the pace of clouds or even weeds,
The window murmurs lightly to the vacant room,
And seems as if it commented with mild surprise
On some arrival, timely or unique;
Slow by the rapid stream, perhaps, or quick in the slow
skies.

Why does the window murmur—and to whom?
What notable event does it report
That's far above the heads of furniture,
Nor heeded by the absent-minded room?

Is it first cuckoo-fall?—the double word
Dropping like seed into the wood, instant with Spring?

Or is it rose-fall?—end of the first rose,
Spilled from the hand of Summer, pensively?

Perhaps first apple-fall?—scatter and thud,
And Autumn here that moment, cornucopia slanted?

Or is it only the first snow-fall?—one,
One, and then one, slid furtive down, as if
Winter himself had thought the moment haunted?

Windows look out of rooms at poetry,
That pours back through them, lyrical in birds,
Epic in weather, narrative in streams;

And looking out seem half-aware of someone
Shadowed behind them, borrowing their eyes.

O window, when you murmur, 'Only look!'
Don't ask who listens now. Never inquire
Why soundlessness should grow into a habit,
Helpless and final as the dust.
                                        Suppose
She may be resting yet in the great bed,
Tuned always to your accent, though her heart
Is listening miles away to mine.—Might she
Not lie so still? Never so long, so still?
Should there, long since, have come to you at least
The flicking over of a page—at least
Her busy pencil, whispering word by word
The letter she would send—at very least
A sigh?
                                        So would she sigh,
In the dark ages of an afternoon,
When you would draw her to some poetry
(Fall of the word, the rose, the fruit, the fleeting crystal),
So would she sigh a war away—since tears,
If tears were let, would rain away the world:
Sigh in the great bed for its emptiness,
The waste of poetry, the waste of years.

The Shape of a Bird

'Break off your argument,
Dearest of patient friends, with whom
I have turned this windless wood
To a long, carpeted room,
Hearing you always invent
New cures for a sickly mood.
Drop your eyes to the floor:
We have strolled, you see, by accident
To a corner we missed before.—
What do you see with your
Imaginative eye?'

'Feathers—a circle of grey:
Little arena empty of strife:
Some murdered ring-dove. Why?—
Very well! I see the way
Death is haunted by life:
A circle of feathers keeping
Vaguely the shape of a bird,
Though, at mere thought of a wind's creeping,
Each could be separately stirred,
The whole image blurred—
What would you have me see?'

'A man and his children keeping
Vaguely the shape of a family still,
When the meaning is lost that she
Alone could give to that word.

Or again, that man alone,
Keeping by effort of will
The shape of the self she freed,
Like the shape of a lost, migratory bird.
With all coherence gone.
With moods that one by one
To the wind's humour succeed.'

To the Crater

Sometimes at nudge of day,
Recalled from inconsequent sleep,
There at the moment of truth,
There in the bird-nibbled grey
One is back—fastened again
To the lip of disaster, appalled,
Staring down into absence, a gap
Where the courts of true living should be,
Where the feared and unfaceable thing
Came to pass, and the city flew up
In a spasm of dust, and the losing
Sea toppled in like a wall.

'It has happened.' Mute the response
To that world-altering wreck.
Cry of no tongue, no sound,
Gone out, unanswered, echoless
Over unbeing: as once,
In the crisis of time; but the moment
Is always the same; there is only
The cry neither uttered nor drowned
By the silence. The single event
Reverberates always; and there,
Once there, the will is to stay
Always—where the torn pavement
Ends, and the final tree

Hangs horizontal in air.

But time draws one back to the text
Of the day and its duty, affirms
The transcendence of life in the moment,
This moment, the next, and the next.

But the will is perverse: to remain
Astounded; surveying the city
In memory; measuring good
By the loss of it; clinging to pain.

But time is tenacious, the great
Healer cannot fail at his task.

But, granted the primal unkindness,
Unkindness can be what you ask.

Before a Sleep

I am still looking, my dear.
I stand at an upper window,
This night of incipient Spring,
In a strange house, before sleep,
In the world we both called 'here'.
I use eyes for us both:
Lovable ordinariness
I look for, peering deep.

I see burn from a cloud
A moon rimmed like a shilling;
Shadow's ink on a lawn;
A long wood's hairy line.
Using ears for us both,
I hear a dog, then cars,
Hear an elm-tree filling
With warm dark wind of growth.

Soon—for what isn't soon,
In the long-drawn yawn of the stars,
That happens on earth?—looking
Will end. Spring nights will keep
The floating round of a moon
In my absence. Perhaps one waking
To watch-dog or deep-breathing tree
May think of you briefly, then sleep.

Later, but soon, there'll remain
Nothing. All of you gone;
Name, nature, story expunged;
With all that joy, all the pain.
We might not have known the extreme
Awareness of love. It will be,
Through time, as though we had not—
Incredible though it must seem

To one who stands in his flesh,
Tuned to a warm night window,
Living hands on rough paint:
With the whole sense of you beating
A pulse in darkness—with fresh,
Then faint, your love like a wind
Which falling and rising will always
Motion the buds of one mind.

Hotel Bedroom

Tenderness of evening sky: the light shrinking,
The mirror lifting a dulled eye to the cornice.
Breath of a city: multitude of delicate sounds
Off an unfamiliar horizon; the blind-cord stirring
Unevenly, a pendant on the breast of twilight.

We have slept for some minutes, I discover—resuming
now
In a room shades darker; and lie together, inert
In a kind of atonement, desire left to sleep on,
Almost like a bed-fellow, a third. And we,
In a moment of unsought grace, perfectly rhyming
together,
A kind of plenary indulgence, are excused
All inquietude, all anxiety; and take pleasure
In the silhouette of the wardrobe—observing, too,
How the basin taps are marvellously defined
By twin faint stars. And meditate on the world
Beyond these murmuring horizons, where nations await
No judgement, only sentence—our world being,
This moment, small and safe in a hired room,
And this nude room as rich to explore as the world.

The luggage waits to be opened on the stool.
The floor-boards speak discreetly in the corridor.
The cord moves, pendant in the rhythm of compassion.

We shall never lie here again. Already the room
Overlooks our one-night tenure; vacantly exists

For tomorrow, always for tomorrow; hears already
The rapid portering footsteps pause, and drop their
    burden;
Then the brisk engagement of the lock—sees
Faces, not ours, that enter glancing around them
The same unspoken comment: 'Here, the exception.
This will never be home.' We are virtually gone
    already—
Might almost never have come. We moved too lightly
Through the public mind of this room—appeared too
    briefly
In the long exposure of the dark impersonal lens,
To be more, in that darkening eye, than ghosts.

Tenderness of the fugitive; of the immaterial;
Of the soon-deleted; of the fond once-in-a-while.
Of a blind-cord moving, softly, softly,
In time with the low breathing of maternal twilight.
Of rhyming together, once in an endless while.

Near as Near

Sentenced to death for the mere act of breathing:
To find adjacent cells, what luck that is,
For strangers, if with marked affinities!
Each to the other all he owns bequeathing.

These two, and in the dark hours best of all,
Would lie and have their hearts knock messages,
Near as they could be through the bone-hard wall.

Jay's Feather

Emergent out of a hill simple as childhood
Moving always downwards deftly downwards
Grooving woods with self-delighted being
While urgent on its devious way to some
Repose   or different being different motion
Rounding a known corner a certain ash-tree
Sounding like pent laughter in private talk
It flows to its one moment of recognition
Seen   prized   actual   brilliant   pure
Reflecting her face who rests on a rail of the bridge
Projecting into it all the love which moves
Green through her mind   and letting a jay's feather
Slipped from her fingers waft and be twitched away
Gripped and drowned in other darker reflections

Liquid Time

They stand on the one-plank bridge, mother and boy,
To hear the bell and the dark voice in the flow;
And the child in the wonder of it forgets his toy;
And the mother remembers one who went to comply
With a call to arms, laughing and leaning so,
As if beyond all partings life must be gay;
Then the child out of its dream says 'water going by',
And drops a leaf in, and shows it twirling away.
But the mother sees liquid time going by: she thinks
Time emptying, time taking my youth.
Yet time brought me my joy—all misery shrinks
To a point beside that. Now we are just in our prime.
All shall be well if only (please God) it's the truth
That when the parting's done there will still be time.

A Box of Beads

Imagine, I said, there truly were ample time,
And I, stooping to the floor like this, could afford
To lose myself in these scattered beads which I'm
Retrieving, could take up and examine each one,
Live it with finger and thumb and put it away,
Until it would seem an entire life-time were done
In beads, dull, bright or middling, like day after day,

Certain that when at last I straightened up stiff,
On the far side of the table you would still
Be watching the same chance pattern of rooks on the hill,

And all our promised morning barely begun.

A Passing Likeness

I glance through the steamy photographer's window-
   pane
At a smile like yours: too quick, my gullible mind
Leaps to the joy of you, sharp, authentic again!

Not really like at a second look; yet behind
The gay expression, surely the self must be,
In some sense one could learn, your copy—at least, of
   your kind?

So I grope for this unknown girl, in the rooms that she
Calls home, I question her voice, views, notion of fun;
While a drop zig-zags on the pane dispiritingly.

Utterly, utterly someone else.—Beyond measure
Remote is she, in the glow of a prime just begun,
From the long-since cold, untraceable girl I treasure,
Who was among semblances truth, among many the
   one.

After a Fashion

He used to think her mode set up a norm,
Girls being meant by history to look so—

Knew fashion reached in her its ultimate form:
Short skirts but flared, a coloured mouth to mean
More clearly what it meant, and hair to flow
Swept back from brow to nape in natural curls.

Long afterwards—when first young eyes were seen
Dingy as shopman's dummies, much too dark;
Lips natural, much too pale—he pitied girls
Their slavery, and great cupolas of high hair.

But young girls give the arbitrary the mark
Of the ineluctable by merely being.
One day when leafing through an album where
Her looks were final beyond change or doubt,

He saw how she, who'd made, had kept his seeing.
Already, though not far, she had receded
To where true beauty's neither in nor out,
And Nefertiti smiles. Then he was glad.

Then he whose wish had been to die when she did
Observed that, in a fashion, so he had.

Life is a Rembrandt

One time of grace,
And all the rest an angry muddle of effort:
Effort to find oneself in the right place;
Anger to find in life's vague hall of mirrors
No mirror framing the right face.

One shaft of glory,
And all before a darkness, and all after
A dimness, not so dark but that a hoary
Glimmer excites it from that urgent scene
Which holds the highlight of the story.

Life is to tease.
Life is a hint, a parable, a preview.
Life is a Rembrandt, where the Painter sees
Great procreative darkness big with light;
And there's no meaning unless darkness please.

The Bright Cloud

In this warmed valley,
Rich after the sun,
Strange brightness lasted
A long while on.

Grief, the bright cloud,
Charged it with radiance,
Festive, in a way,
As long spent day.

You stood in that colour,
Pensive, motionless:
I knew the doves and hands
Of your once wedding dress.

Your eyes a shadow,
Hands in mine,
Stillness the one sign,
And in your gaze also.

Long I scanned your gaze,
Found in its shadowing
All of anguish guessed,
And in your watching, rest.

Long I had your smile,
Pitying, gentle-eyed;
Rested in your nearness,
Long after you died.

Radiance decays;
The woods dissolving
Grow aloof and dumb,
And the dew, numbing.

The bright cloud will tarnish.
Losing you and finding,
Earnestly I trace
On nothingness your face,

Trusting you to treasure
The good thing begun;
To mean, in separation,
What we learnt as one.

But hands loosen,
Your fingers, withdrawn,
Brush to the tips of mine,
Touch—touch—and are gone.

Hunger's End

On the night platform Luck and I
Walked up and down. I did not know
At first that it was Luck nor why
Encountered here, although

I knew an inescapable choice
Hung in the balance, he betraying
An urgency in frown and voice
That stressed the option. He was saying,

'On? Or return? Which? Time's run out
To its last ticking. Death's as near
As signalled. Notice, if you doubt,
Our unambiguous venue!' Here

He waved towards the lamplit fence
Between us and numb night's abyss.
Letters, grime darkened but immense,
Spelt HUNGER'S END. 'It comes to this:

'Your life, but all your life, again,
With every moment memory shrinks
From counting: shame, deceit, and pain,
(I choose the part which might, one thinks,

'Be best rubbed out for ever). Or
The next, the other . . .' And here a hand
Gestured into the darkness for
Elucidation. So I scanned

That darkness. Narrowing out of sight,
The line curved somewhat round—to judge
From four reflected threads of light
In the obscurity. A smudge

Of light lay over them—but far,
Far distant—a faint beam, a kind
Of cindery undulating bar
Drawn out (or so it came to mind)

Along some ridge of hills. But whether
News of the moon, or mirrored tint
Of all the arc-lit streets together
Of one great city, or else a hint

Of earth-occluded dawn, which burned
Absolute in some other place
Unknown, I could not tell; but turned
To that sly prodigal faithless face.

'She whom I loved—she whom I love
Years deep in abject death—who was,
Who will be that to which I move
In this or any world, because

'That is my truth, and heaven must be
Wherever our two joys can touch
In greeting, one the other: she
Whom you, divine dear Luck, with such

'Marvellous caprice, once lightly gave
Me, undeserving in despair—
What hope of the one end I crave,
Rapture of recognition—there?'

'I know nothing of hope,' Luck said,
'Chances are my wares'—muttering
Abstractedly with lifted head,
'Chances enough hold everything.'

Once more my staring found its mark
Of faint equivocal dawn, and then
Ranged up into the answerless dark.
It was the very moment when,

Floating conspicuous in the sky
(Yet till that moment hardly seen),
One bloodshot, minatory eye
Blinked, and was perilous green.

Nothing ensued. No bell. No twitch
Of mile-long nerves. Both platforms stood
In shabby relaxation, which
Was torment in itself. Or could

The ear detect something, indeed?—
Far back, in dull remoteness drowned,
Mumbling and whispering in its speed
With overtaking its own sound,

Enormity bore down—with roar,
Even then, of brakes, with shuddered ground,
With great pale squares of light: and bore
Down, jarring, dumbly: to dumbfound:

To deafen: oh, to surge away
(Passed, glittering, on the other track)
Into the utterly new, the grey
Proffer of that horizon. 'Back!'

I whispered, catching at Luck's sleeve.
'I choose, I choose! The past again,
With all the ignoble things you grieve
To count, the ignominy, the pain.

'Her love redeems it all, our heaven
Was there, but snatched away. Restore
That taste—the very moments given—
The crumbs we had: I ask no more.'

Luck groaned aloud. His lifted chin
Showed the shut eyelids in the glow
Of the last platform lamp, drawn thin
Over that odd young countenance. 'So!

'And this the same lamp, the same sky;
And those your words, or some such words . . .
How many times must you and I
Meet on these hapless boards!'

Something was Wrong

Love always knew
His drift would be distorted.
In moments when
His signal came most clear—
When talk grew deep,
Or when exchange of glancing
Seemed like the drop
That stars a leaf of grass;
When music paused,
Poised on its own carved wind—
The talk tailed off,
The star shrank in shadow,
The music hung
Like hawks to fall away.
The note of end,
The prick of end, the whisper
Of end, of end,
Perplexed and numbed the air.

And yet, and yet,
With every fleeting rapture
Love wrung his hands
To be so misconstrued;
And grieved to know
His perfect notions cancelled;
And sent his grief
In signals to them both:
'Something is wrong!
I did not mean each blessing
To shine and die,

I did not mean in sequence,
I did not mean
Profusion to mean loss.
Something is wrong:
Any day's death is wrong.
I spell Rejoice,
And still you read Goodbye!'

Daybreak and Paradigm

Why did they call us away
From what was enough in itself—
A thrush in the crack of day,
A primrose tilting a leaf:
Meaning enough, one would say—
And where were they calling us to?

Often, behind the wild word
In the narrow green tension of dawn,
Was the voice we would surely have heard
That moment, if this had been mute.
But when we might hear—when the bird
Stopped—there was only the dawn.

Often, between the wild face
And our zeal, was the absolute flower
That shines in no temporal place.
One moment it beckoned, and then
There was only the scent and the grace
Of the casual, vanishing flower.

They seemed only imaged in Time
To draw us beyond—where they are.
And we, who perceived the sublime
But in echoes and glimpses, must wait—
Like a stanza awaiting a rhyme,
Uncompleted, left open to God.

So they'd sing and they'd shine, would rejoice
Two Aprils at once, with an air
Of saying mere petals and voice
Could slip out of Time when they chose . . .
Would that I now had the choice,
To break the grave dream, and be there!

Under the Breath

Listen. Come close.
Laugh in my mind if ever I
Grow old and morose!

Give me the low cue
For gratitude, when I lag
Not thinking of you;

But do not count much
On gifts meagre without
Your energizing touch.

Only in all seasons
Move me to work new praise
For the old reasons.

In the Autumn rain,
What you said of burrowing
Through time, say again.

Sometimes what you said
Walks like Christ to sanctify
The Pit in my head.

Show wild daffodils!
Touch me to the quick with gleams
Of our five Aprils.

Be—no sound—the bright
Audible silence sharing
My tipped lamp at night.

Touch with forgiving
Hand in darkness—as you did
When you were living.

Enough

Matins is over, then. I hear
The sermon-silence give, at last.
They rise to music, but appear
To find it taken a shade fast.
Still onward, out of step, they plod,
        Until 'O God
Our help in ages past' is past.

The seesaw hymn, the rasping psalm
Have stretched bucolic hands to shed
(More moving as their gift) some balm
Where this humped, eye-bright quilt is spread;
As though the form in this deep cot
        Were you, and not
Your clothes deceptive in your bed.

Dear one, the time is long, and yet
Not rugged, rather smooth than rough.
I love to tell you this, who set
My good before all ends. The stuff
Of life is coloured by your love,
        And still can prove
Pleasant enough, pleasant enough.

Reveries around Eurydice

I

And yet for Orpheus it was not so bleak
If he heard even one footfall far behind;
For when he turned and she was utterly gone,
His woe knew she existed. He could seek
Still the sweet, forfeited, absolute reward,
Which, one day, somewhere, he would find.
Oh for some evidence of a step—not heard
Only down echoing galleries of the mind!

II

You would have followed without puzzle or fret,
With death-drugged irises trustful, and no sound;
Safe in the recognition of a silhouette,
Sure of a back, fixed on a style of walking . . .
But that old legend is the wrong way round!

I am the one who follows; and I detain,
I doubt, I agitate. Am I supposed to learn,
From something wholly beneficent and made plain
Even in the quality of your silence, never,
For both our sakes, to even wish you'd turn?

III

Suppose an Orpheus who is always turning,
And a Eurydice no sooner gone
Than drawn by remote tenderness; and yearning
To whisper in an ear still deaf, though burning,
Just to keep moving, to plod on!

IV

Now there is only following to be done.
Make no distinction. Say: one follows one.
So figures in some fresco may perplex,
Too small for age to be discerned, or sex.
But here on hills we note them; there again—
One far behind—marked on a twilight plain.
Surely (but this the painter does not treat)
In some auspicious grove at last they meet?
There, in his secret vision clearly seen,
They are already, and have always been:
Standing like lovers, face to mirrored face,
Through one infinity of reflected grace;
Or strolling side by side like friend with friend
Who find each other in some common end.

At Lengthening Range

Wait for me in that other mode of being,
Where waiting is no word, for Time is out.
Recall that since you died I have been seeing
Things of no brilliance: if I grope in doubt,
Be patient for a while, and let me trace
Truth—as blind fingers reconstruct a face.

Be slow to flash with unpredicted pleasure,
Lovely, impetuous, welcoming one—be slow
Even to remind. Dull, let my dullness treasure
Some instance of contentment long ago,
When the mere drip-drop of the rain could bless.
Point the safe context in lost happiness!

Small need for such a tact when first you died!
I safely could have joined you anywhere:
Turned at a sound, and simply laid aside
Both book and grief, because you waited there.
The days were full of doors through which you might
Come back, before the failing of the light . . .

How bright the land of loss!—inviting, too:
As though the land of having were extended
Through one vast gap of unimagined view
To the world's end, could such a world be ended—
A sunlit, bruised, and thunder-blotted moor
It seemed mere chance we could not both explore.

And yet, it seemed, we did. A prospect so
Prodigious, full of meaning, and exalted,
Told me you saw, unseen. I felt it grow,
As climbers—on from where they briefly halted—
Feel challenge bud through skylines, dark and vast,
Strangely transforming even the sunlit past.

Oh, that was the early, easy time when you,
Still near, were all but actual among those
Blizzards of loss friends hope to see one through.
(No wind more welcome out of darkness blows.)
All gave the succour, then, grief had not craved.
But when you died indeed, they said, 'he's saved.'

And as you died, year to descending year
It seeped away, beyond all skill to stem—
The life-blood of the things you cherished here.
When they grew cold I would surrender them,
Picture or candlestick or favourite shoes,
For other hands to crack, wear out or lose.

For things receive a glow when love regards them,
A kind of soul, like chattels in a fable,
And keep it, for a while, when love discards them—
Like a warm necklace on a dressing-table.
But when it cools, no taking-thought can add
To cloth or clay the elated look they had.

Treasures that none can touch may seem set fair
To last for ever—till an ageing brain

Sheds them like hair, or colour from the hair.
Lost, before loss can feel the warning pain—
That muddy walk, a joke, a way of greeting,
Some meeting—all the flavour of some meeting.

Paupered by living on, I trust I may
Yet reach our long-appointed rendezvous,
Clutching some icon of our love. But say
Mind falls apart! Then if, quite dead to you,
Dead to your whole existence, worse than blind,
These hands grope forward—be the thing they find.

I Know

In bitter-sweet beginners' days
Before you learnt to love, but jibbed
Or danced in love's magnetic field,
We looked around for things to praise
In common. Once, when I revealed
Some curious, deeply private thought,
You seemed to me clairvoyant—so
Strangely your murmur cut me short:
'I know!'

But in love's candid days ideas
Homed to you of their own accord:
How often I explained some touch,
In book or landscape asking tears—
Or some predicament where I
Needed your laughter for reward—
And then let explanations go,
Forestalled by your perceptive cry,
'I know!'

If heaven allowed in gentleness
Death's freezing solitude to grow
A warm horizon of your arms,
First there, in them, I should confess
All that was wretched, weak and low;
And hear before the worst was out
(Sweet beyond grief for your distress)
Two words again outstrip my thought:
'I know.'

This Wood for Context

What if earth
Be but the shadow of heav'n; and things therein
Each to other like?

PARADISE LOST, V. 574

Low sun; high summer; and no stir;
No quiver in all the painted trees,
Not one—though with a day's great warmth
A river darkens on.

I enter woods where, growth being slow,
Time seems to hold its breath, and up
The centre of this watchful room
Climb the steep, memoried path.

A sense of wariness prevails.
From folds unseen the fret of lambs,
Intense yet tranquil, drugs the mind
And holds it, wide-asleep.

Listening, that robin is—like one
Who's diligent to note, far off,
Whistled rejoinder, snap of twig:
More vigilance than tune.

About I face, and listen too.
Now high once more the leaf-locked sun
Gives out bewildering threads of shine
That ply and throb and wheel.

The inclination is to stare.
Those granulated rays that still
Shrink to their centre or dilate
Dandle the mind. But now

The brighter lamp is flashed below,
Redoubled on the scrawling flood:
A whiter sun from there beats up,
Being troubled with its glass.

I turn to mount once more, and see
Light's after-image dance ahead
Through fern and bramble up to where
One shaft of sunlight points

To the dark hairpin-bend above.
Odd, though, how much of lustre seems
To mark the air itself, and not
Each row of prescient stems.

It seems curiously framed—and meant:
The plush of amber gloom, the spots
And gleams of floating brilliancy:
A hushed, but vacant, stage.

Suppose an actor!—There could be
The slimmest creature stationed there,
Where those drawn-over roots recall
A mimic Prospero's cave.

As though that fancy gave the cue,
This figure see descending now,
Slow through the picked-up lights towards
That bigger 'spot' mid-way!...

Feminine, rapt in vision, still
Youthful, but with a grace that seems
Remembering, or inhabiting,
Some truth beyond surmise.

Hand stretched towards me. False no more
The theatre's lovely more-than-life.—
Miranda to her Ferdinand.
Beatrice beyond the stream.

Long thighs that flow in the flared skirt,
Tall brow, curl-swept to shoulder square,
With eyes too blessed for me to know
Where now they look for home;

With traits that stab the memory's quick!
With flesh, most tangible flesh! Like truth
That gaze—too deep, to more than skim
The mesh of meanings hidden ...

Suppose, my wandering mind, suppose
It proved no day-dream, but Heaven's way
To close the wound that gaped when she
Was moved to that sharp death.

Suppose when I have died myself—
I still unconscious of my death—
She glows into my sight, beyond
The skill of dreams to fake.

Picture the proof of her: a twig
Snapped sharply into moss—O sudden
Stricture of the breath!—a fern
Trapped in her passing hand.

One thrill of fear—imagine that!—
Shy of the very end I crave!
And still to hear her breathe my name,
And die into her love.

Dear wood, known path, remembered sun,
Now veiled beyond recall today,
It could be! Will on neither side
Has failed: this do I know.

Obscurely in your gloom, repeated
Somewhere in heaven, such joy might spring.—
Surely a context might be given
To spare my death-dulled sense?

Surely, old haunt-of-ours, you could
Be looking-glassed in Paradise,
Purely to spare my heart, which even
Shook when we met on earth?

If so, it might then seem to me
(Confused a little by my death),
As though we'd merely drawn apart—
And mused—and then resumed.

On some hot night, years back, your slope
Caused us to halt, dead-still—and learn
(Come to ourselves once more) we had
Paused longer than we knew.

The Green Beard

The summered sea, the lazy lazuli,
And she singing a song that had no ending.

The sea was glances of a rapturous eye,
The combe secret. Over the headland, hawks
Trembled like heat; and near her lover bending
Over his page, she sang their state of bliss.

Naked she sang, twisting convolvulus stalks
For a round garland, shadowing her breasts.
Dragonflies flickered between this and this
Pure pleasure, and the conscious waters glanced.

She sang of some great light which never rests
From wings, and laughter vaulted through the sea.
(Far out, the arches of her dolphins danced,
Dark, but as lovely as the hawks were light.)

She sang because he sang in her, and she
Was he, and all was glancing to their joy—
And with her fingers combed one moist and bright
Grass beard that from a rock flowed motionless.

She knew their Eden easy to destroy,
And indestructible too. She was to lie
Through nights of dread and inwardly caress
That beard—with all her peace on this depending:

The summered sea, the lazy lazuli,
And she singing the song that had no ending.

A Closing Music

So music flowed for them, and left
The silence brimmed.

Music took charge that evening, and with deft
Flights into rhapsody, a clarinet
Sang of their passion—while a candle slimmed,
The window had its fingering of dark rain.

It was not music chosen to forget
The separation and the pain to come:
It caught the separation and the pain
Into the high dark of its tender dance.

Firelight and candlelight and rain were dumb
(Which often spoke their moods for them) to speak
This exaltation. Soft in stare and glance,
These waited for the music to say all.

And three times through a falling air would break
Such tenderness—such pity—of dark strings,
It could have been surmised there would befall
Something, not faced, but fingered round by doubt.

And it was death, and it was death, that things
Meant all that time. And love's one world was cleft
From top to bottom. All their lights gone out,
Their praises to the god of joy, all hymned.

Music had flowed in them. It left
The silence brimmed.

The Unforeseeing

There it was, chalk-white, when they came to the
brow and looked over:
Starred in the dark combe, only not, as once,
A mere White Dwarf of a house—more a Supernova
Beaming back that this was the new home.
And the rooms genial, quick with an apt response
To each fancy formed for the months ahead:
Packing conjectural honey fast in the comb,
Little enough they glimpsed actualities there.
See them, rich in their dream, imagining bed,
Imagining stocked larder and pictured wall,
While seated on grocery box and bottom stair:
Little enough they guessed the dream inexact,
Such fancies fated to look like nothing at all—
Beside the felicity broached that morning, the fact.

Invisible She

Once while I stared from that transfigured crest
Down into evening through deceptive shine,
Invisible she below the shadow-line
Prepared the perfect supper-dish, I guessed.
Suddenly I saw the little house possessed
By agitations of an inward vine
That speared through eaves and window-panes to twine
And twinkle here and there in smothering zest.
This was no premonition of decay.
Who ever saw soft-fingered ruin poke
Through glass intact, or elegiac spray
Run spiral up a column of blue smoke?
I always said the house must find a way
To celebrate her living there, or choke.

The Pattern

Night the hand that swayed the auspicious stars,
Night the stream's voice, passionately kind;
Dawn a face beyond the casement bars,
Face of a tall hill touselled round with dew;
Morning all open, open to the mind
In one white page time would not turn again;
Noon, a pause—life's pattern full in view
Below the oak-bough with the bread and wine.
Afternoon then for flesh to entertain
Mind in some homely or adventurous fashion;
Dusk a brown moth called by candleshine
Under a hill still topped with saffron day;
Night, and the always of that voiced compassion;
Night of the good stars, never meant to stay.

This

In the black sunlight of sleep,
In the white night of the pleasured
Spirit and flesh made one,
Her hand found out his hand,
Leaf-shape leaf-shape of bone,
Took the dry fit of it quick,
The strong interstices measured,
Knowing—as instantly known.

Their lips said little then—
Nothing of consequence.
But what each hand beat out
In the code of the pulsing heart
Came clear enough as to sense.

'This', said one hand, 'is true'.—
'This is true, beyond doubt'.—
'Out of the whirlwind of time
In the cold hole of the stars,
A hand shapes to a hand'.—
'Which, being brought about,
Is out, like an uttered word'.—
'Never can not have occurred'.—
'This'.—'And the knowledge of this'.

The ears on the pillow heard,
But being sun-drenched with sleep
And conscious of nothing amiss,
Hardly more than one word,
This . . . this . . . this . . .

Dark to Dark

When darkness in their widening pupils grew
As darkness in the room grew round and slow
Darkness dissolved all prudent thoughts and drew
Doubtful conclusions from all forms and when
Amorous darkness a wished vertigo
Toppled two silences towards one thought
Which only flesh can think, O softly then
Lights were struck up and lights began to swim
And wicks to ripen wide, candles were caught
And swept upstairs with sidelong eyes to touch
Highlights on fallen silk and tumbled limb
And shine and be forgotten and grow shorter.
Then darkness entered new—not new so much
As come from far, with owls and travelling water.

In Secret

What fills the darkness now but gratitude
For such a present as her perfect love
Given free away, and by the act renewed
With greater zest for unimagined giving;
Because her will is always to improve
The joy that in each mood or mode she brings—
Who says that having touched this kind of living
No separation could make either lonely.
What sings, though dark? It is the blood that sings!
Somewhere a dog keeps on. Somewhere perhaps
A war keeps on: our window-catch is only
Tuned to talk peace. Think at a door somewhere
The World, that worried secretary, taps
And is at once called in. Not now. Not here.

The Set for the Play

Rooms in provincial hotels, war's odd oases,
Prim caves for exotic embraces,
Love's interchangeable cells, with only a number
For name, and just the distinction between
Dull '20', defiant '13', and dependable '4',
To hint there are niceties even in commonplaces;
That you cherish, and always will,
Some idiosyncrasies which you believe to be graces,
And claim that nowhere else can the world be seen
Quite the same, as by walking across to your sill,
And pushing aside the dainty muslin screen—

Below in the cat-crossed yard
A man was unloading a dray,
Engaged in some private charade
Of revolving a barrel away—
As like to himself as a print
Of a man unloading a dray.
Late afternoon had begun
Browning the varnish of air
To a ripe old-masterly tint.
The top of the sash in the sun
Felt hot to the fingers. And there,
Just at one end, by the cord—
The sign we might have expected:
The indicative relic, the one
Sly-blue, wafer-thin blade,
Overlooked by the prying or bored
Archaeological maid:
Significance quickly detected!

It established that primitive man
Camped here before us—even skilled
In his troglodyte way. We began
To envisage his few gruff wants
(Largely, no doubt, unfulfilled):
To picture how gamely he wrung
Small comforts out of the milieu:
To question, indeed, the response
One would get even now by ringing.
Then the squeal of the sash upflung
On a clatter of plates and singing;
And beyond that, bright as lobelia,
Jeans on a neighbouring line,
Wind-sculpture in clean relief
(Nine men's morris a-row
With twirl of a white handkerchief).
Somewhere, the moo of a cow.
Somewhere, invisible hay.
And all, lit with divine
Felicity—lit, in some way—
Flood-lit from behind or above,
Like stage scenery which has
No function but to be gay—
Like the scenery it actually was:
Being but the back-cloth of love,
Being but the set for the play.

Do you guess, bare rooms—respectable, too, however:
Quite, like a poor dress-maker, freshly turned out,
With your toilet-table not square, but across the corner,
The diagonal posture being refined, without doubt;
With your mirror too pinched in the oval, and a notice
there

To say that meals can never be brought to you, never—
Do you guess, undernourished rooms, that you may be
    immortal?
Remember an afternoon you were swept off your feet
To join in the laughter of Always, your true lover?
No, you remember nothing, and guess nothing.
No. One day is another. Each day is complete,
When you, having heard the tooth-brush rattle next
    door,
Cling tight, in the snap of the dark, to your
    self-possession;
But relax, in a little, even your faint expression
Of '6', or magical '7', or trustworthy '4'.

Keeping Engagements

Threading the human thicket of our city,
Down streets, rank with faces, hastening on,
Resolute, inconspicuous, unremarked—
Suddenly perceiving in the awkward space
Between two blocks (waste-pipes and ventilators),
All shall be well!

Why then—why miracle of dateless then—
Realisation explodes like a street-band and
A kind of glory is flung storey to storey,
A kind of ditty has given rhymes to the city;
For if all shall be, even at the final dot
Of time's immense perspective—final dots
Where it breaks off, our sad passage of time—
Why then all is, here, now, by implication:
The secret out, the simple truth proclaimed
In these damp canyons of complexity
Where roots of care twist faces.

Tremble, great window glass. Click, door. Change, red,
To green approval. Stagger on again,
Sleep-walking traffic. Certain passers-by,
Cut off remarks
And let them float to fade in the grey wind.
You there, spent matches,
Form in that angle of the dingy plinth
A civilization's minute monogram.
Excellent City, in your cares and methods
Be anything you will, or what you are—

And still be praised, forgiven, relished,
Accepted and reprieved, for all
Gratuitousness of mere diversity!

Gripping the amulet, hope,
The sacred pebble in the secret palm,
Threading, all but invisible, the way
Of cherished obscurity—here step
Deftly aside—here halt
Expressionless with several by the bollard,
Judging the moment to proceed.

Morning somewhat advanced,
Customary with engagements,

Light rain resuming,

White sky to westward,

Smell of the wet streets.

Three O'Clock

Hesitate with letters, there by the pillar-box,
Holding the gesture. Listen: from a great tower,
Implied among the houses, there falls the first
Portentous gold initial of Three o'clock,
Stamped on the afternoon. At once, a voice
Comes through in your mind, and vanishes: 'It is the hour
Of—' But of what? Plainly, no passer-by
Tuned to that imperative message. You watch the wind
Tumble the smoke, lift half the blossom of a tree,
Twitching away April like a table-cloth.
Sparrows occur. Wheels twinkle. Thin and high,
High and continuing high like a violin—
A vapour trail describes an enormous flower,
Grown out, nudging the blue, into absolute silence.

Why so happy? Now, while the tower involves
The town in tone—now in the power of Three—
To observe felicity! To watch it flow
Into all manner of articulateness, and as though
Inventing even more than invading vapour or tree—
A cloud, a wheel, a sparrow, a lifted tree.
Stand with your post neglected. It will only seem
From the correct day's register of enterprise
One comma dropped, in the end. But joy is rare.
It is most easily evaded, being extreme.
Tricked brain, surrender to it! Concentrate, eyes,
On that one budding-point of the mottled sky's,
Where, reverent as laughter, holy as vanity,
Everything and utterly nothing flowers in the air!

Ideogram

Grass, of a long wet morning down a wall,
Received the sunlight with a sharp impact
As they sat still, and let the engine stall,
Tasting the cold green silent smell of rain,
And shut one eye to make a drop refract,
And heard the tick of metal as it cooled,
Knowing their luck—its quiddity made plain
In each bright ideogram of wayside grass.
Something there was in grass that overruled
And flourished commonsense, the way it curled,
Then shone their glory back like looking-glass:
It was so very there—express—and free—
It was obscure like them, and by the world
As unobserved as they could hope to be.

Driving Westwards

See the gold cock and four swart pinnacles
Poke out of pasture as the lane loops over,
Till distance with a long blue drink of hills
Comes in one mouthful, but things supervene,
A chapel, a child, a hawk, a smell of clover,
And now all's lost in downwardness, a drop
Through trunks like faint hurrahs, an echoing screen
To a small bridge, curious with ferns. Here stop.
Be in the sense of this cool place. Be here.
Be this particular here—it knows one way,
By green and brown, to write our meaning clear.
You who beside me down the roads of bliss
Make any place we greet on such a day
Conclusive utterance of our love, make this.

The Appointment

Going upstairs to room white as my mood,
Going by narrow window, what halts the foot?
A dark bird flowing under a bright hill
Has caught me, fast in thought.

Flies live in the darkness over that water,
Where the bough bends forward, slow, as in recollecting.
Clouds in their tender brightness move on that hill.
And when the window moves, a hinge tightens a fist.
I see! And momently life becomes larger-than-life,
    looming
As a face looms on the screen to convey a meaning,
And I say to myself (watching a wave in the stream
All the while flashing and flickering a secret message at
  someone)
So! You are here.
It is here, then, once more, the occult appointment is
    kept.
Yet (catching no word of that message),
Yet who (looking up in despair
To a mark on the wall like a colon—clearly a sign to
  someone),
Who are you?

From the candid stare, in the white mood of the house,
No answer. Though it might have been given, perhaps,
Far off, where something sparked in the sky, turning.
But oh, beyond reading faint: no more to be understood
Than the playground's wind-rubbed cry.

Emptied of knowing, poured out,
Consumed away, weightless, volatile,
Stooping by the sill, transparent and simple as water,
All at once (as the hill swells into light,
As the clouds move white circles over the hill,
As the bough lifts, lifts, like a face reminded),
I am charged with the mere knowledge of being. I know
That I am. Gratuitous beyond explanation,
I receive this present of a moment. The hill (shrunk again):
Ineffaceably mine! The gift of one cloud! And this hinge!
This encounter, unique and irrevocable, with a hinge!

And if one didn't remember, and just in time,
That after all one is only acting the part of day-dreamer,
One would surely explode into a million particles of joy.

What can one do—but turn away into doing,
As if nothing were extraordinary, or ever mattered at all?

Conscious Light

One field beneath the flying sun grows bright,
Seems held for recognition, and let lapse.
You'd say that field was being thought by light.
Perhaps earth is what light reflects on, thinking
This field—that clump—those cottages. Perhaps
The dark areas live in the same mind,
Only not thought, put by, patiently shrinking
Back into darkness, reconciled though blind.
See how it skims the river to our shore:
Watch the pear-tree jump to it, just as though
What blossoming meant had never been shown before.
Look, the hedge—your hair—O glory explaining
How heaven, for a flash, is fact more than we know.
Now it translates us, now we are the meaning.

A Reading

We read the lights, the coloured lights of summer;
We watch a certain field far in the plain
Turn glassy, chosen by the sun this moment
To illustrate some aspect of young corn.
All round us fields interpret or grow dimmer,
Out to the horizon's sharply-moulded rim,
Red soil, yellow mustard, quarry and segment
Leaded with earth-walls dark to that clean rim.
We read a window for a perfect world,
The stained glass window of a pictured world
Where the good life propounded is no figment;
But, being too near the colours, read askance.
Are we translucent too, like vitreous pigment?
Who can read us and the whole rose at once?

Laughter All Round

When, struggling up, shall we laugh loud at death—
Ours—in two skeletons drawn clean from Earth
For one reminding moment, white like breath
Blown out against the dawn's all-questioning crack,
And find their grin was always meant for mirth,
And see them spread their twenty twigs' applause
At our new-budded ones; then, laughing back,
Vanish a second time? Ah, not for ever!
In some sweet-smelling cupboard hang up yours
Which I laid down with such a dark alas—
Old shape I handled often, but saw never,
Old threadbare thing you'd sigh to thrust away—
Or have her serve us, tibia-deep in grass,
Glad and discreet with the first breakfast-tray.

The Unlit Passage

It still is a May morning.
The shrill gold or aching green
Of beeches coined in, simply, blue
Reaches through the mind and out
To meet young oaks that endlessly
Repeat the strokes of bright and dark:
Tender verticals whose mazes
Render dazzling a delight.
A breeze speaks of pine boughs, only
To tease, because it does not tell
Which way that censer swung.
Stitchwort, and campion,
Five-times-two-point staring stars,
Thrive as all things thrive that are
Live points, or living wicks.
Butterflies in gaps of green
Gutter with low winking lights;
Spider horizontals over
Wider emptinesses, when
Light reveals them, only seem
Slight scratches in green glass;
So the very shadows learn
To flow with light as light with shadow.
And I with busy hand all morning
Lie alert, or lost in thought.

A glance, by prearrangement more than
Chance, it seems, and I observe her
Distant entrance through the non-ex-
Istant wings of that great stage

Lovers feel they act on. Sun
Covers her a moment, stepping
Clear of shadow; again shadow
Here and there along the path
Blinks across her dress; and all she
Thinks of morning and May woods
To meet a lover in, and kneel
To eat and drink in mottled noon
Shows in that blithe, sauntering step,
That goes with sandals and green silk.
Pensively, but with elation
Intensively distilled in grace
Of motion, so she moves, and brings
A notion of life's amplitude,
A sense of shared adventure, both
Immense and secret from the world,
A feel of opening doors that still
Reveal new turns, new passages—
Moves through Summer like a house
And proves it large enough for joy.
Nearer now: the look of greeting
Clearer out of blinded eyes,
Till

Still morning in May it is:
The same morning. If such another
Came, the memory makes them one.
Slender shafts of bright and dark
Engender unifying trances.
Faint brushes far above
Paint the picture of each wind.
Bright is dark is bright though dark.
Light darkens up and up,

Spreads a water, throws a fan,
Shreds and vanishes; and below
Never falters on my arm,
Never alters much, but still
Burns bough-marbled over moss.
Ferns raise their fiddle-scrolls.
All's attending. Willowdown
Falls as only silence falls
Meaningful in crowded rooms
Leaning towards denouement. High,
High the overture, the music:
Fly-music, bird-voices.
I engrossed and still alert.

Glancing I see her, ever the same,
Advancing out of coolness where
Urgent brightness slows the pace,
Emergent from a wall of shadow:
Between the lights in a green dress,
A green dress that extra shadows
Flit across, and so strolling
Lit or lost along the path.
Near next moment—the full mood
Clear in that regardful gaze:
Eyes that read the leaves for pleasure,
Wise with joy's great gravity;
Face that makes of anywhere
A place in poetry and a home.
So she moves. So the moments
Flow to recognition-point,
And then

Again nothing. The picture lost.
The scene put back. Morning it is,
In green or gold of that high sound
Hot with resin. So she enters.

What holds fruition up,
Cheating memory of the simple
Meeting, instant as a smile?

Was there in that wood, not marked
(Because adjacent) by the sunlit
Sunward-gazing eye, some deep
Unlit passage where a yew
Could grow unnoticed, grow sharp-edged
As though cut out of the bright air:
Ragged and irregular hole,
Jagged across Summer?

It was Here

Beech-boles grope with muscular arms of darkness
Crossing out brightness from their own luminous leaves,
The leaves that are strong as faith in their maysilk
    weakness:
They move only as the fingertips of a dancer
Who balancing on the points of a chord achieves
Perpetual repose. On black shadow for ground
The wind-flowers burn with a light denser, intenser,
Just because the negation of all light is so near.—
Surely it was here you stopped when the clue was found,
Watchful with morning eyes where the clearing widens
Into an absolute shining, surely it was here
You saw beyond the riddle the withheld solution?
Twenty and one years deep in the loam of silence,
Silent you stay. Why am I filled with elation?

Intimation

Something was spoken or was left unspoken,
Being said with hands and glances countless times;
For more was meant than came to phrases broken
By the world's pressures or contented sloth.
Something was heard, faint like enormous chimes
Above the traffic—like a delicate sound
In silent rooms—which being caught by both,
Meaning brimmed over, and the world was drowned.
Then something was imagined, so extreme,
So ravishing, of unequivocal worth,
All days home to it on the invisible beam,
All skylines just conceal it, all roads are
Made index-fingers, and the sunflower earth
Sways out of orbit to a mastering star.

The Scent

The scent of joy—
The authentic tang!
Breath taken away,
Thought dislocated:
The past come back
For a tick of the clock,
For a knock of the heart
The past actual:
In the nostril keen
The odd delight:
More pang than pleasure,
More lost than found—
So spiced and wild,
So quick and faint—
The scent of joy!

In the voice recalled
By the right idiom,
In the drawer opened
On the right trinket,
In the old magazine
At the right page,
In the street-lamp's gloss
On the right ivy,
In noon stalking
The right wood—
The scent of joy!

To this, days vanishing
Always point,
Through sins that cloud
That vanishing point;
Through busy pleasure
Deflecting attention,
Through pain requiring
Entire attention;
Through public terror
Touching the sky,
Or private, bending
Over the bed;
Through the street of panic,
Tidal with faces;
Through the unconcern
Of the last ceiling.

Through the fine crack
Of the last skyline:

Known and unknown,
Beyond belief,
Beyond deserving,
Beyond decay,
Beyond description:
The scent of joy!

Triune

What is this truth that set up house in us
When we made one, and seemed to form our third;
Who grew as we have grown by gain and loss,
And knows the road we want but hides the map?
He brought a joy of which we had not heard,
But one so wild it seems a kind of pain;
He brings a pain, now luck runs to a stop,
More to our taste than all joys but his own.
May what he does, through us and by our will,
May what he is, in us and out from us,
Be still the plain truth we were born to tell,
And be said out though none are tuned to hear,
And add its yes to life, a most pure yes,
When no, no, no, grows thick in the world's ear.

A Celebration

Golden and Silver Rains and Falls and Fountains
Brilliant Suns and Stars and Huge Revolving Suns
Rainbow Candles Rainbow Wheels and Showers
Glittering Cascades Glorias and Brilliant Yew Trees

Extravagant their names, unearthly the landskip they furnish,
Where the stars thicken to sunrise, where the suns rise
Plural and bearded, whole oaks come to stature in a moment,
And the twelve-second cherry undresses in a hood of bright rain.

Look how mint the nine worlds were lobbed, how the sheaves
Bowed biblical down. O look how it, how both, how they all
Come gliding up like words in a night of inspiration, and put
Forward elate alternatives, the free inventions of love.

And we with our oohs and ahs in public darkness,
In the doomed harvest of the humble unbuoyant, stand
In the standing corn, are told in the stars. But soon,
Darkness again being ordinary, we drift away.

Turn the night's page, who have written this footnote in
history:
One of our wars is over, someone is crowned, or eighty.
Important eyes have approved the same loud colours.
This moment,
The ones who matter are milling in the awed marquee.

What matters, privately, is this: that homeward we carry
Our prints of another climate, though fading. And some
There are who perceived it, or guessed, or perhaps
remembered;
What it might be, would be (if it ever were feasible): joy.

How Will it Be?

You know how August, like a slant in the light,
Troubles the migratory instinct in whole families:
Away they swerve, each with a private needle
Dancing to some blue end. Toward set of sun
The children weary of counting cars or cats,
Or trying for palindromes in every place-name,
Or trailing hands in speed, that's like a river,
A warm river of boredom, smooth between
The guide-book villages, hazily verified
In three leaps of a look,
Past the hill sarsen, starred by a single glance.
Then they, neglectful of their vow to keep
Watch upon shifty horizons in strict vigil,
Backslide entirely—just as, unobserved,
The downs are shadowing round, and cresting over,
Big with sheer imminence! And thus they have it:
So easy, and all at once, and quite unearned;
So very *gratis*—there, in a final V
Of the crossed skylines, offered like a cup—
The instant recognition of the sea:
Intelligence of the neat, enormous sea:
Burning regard of their importunate sea.

Will it be, like that?—Our homing far from here:
Our joy to which the light is always tilting us?
Not too extreme: not more than we can bear;
Often slighted; and of course unearned; and yet
(All said and done and wept and prayed for)
There?

A Sedative at Daybreak

Here, again!—One splintered second
By the awakening mind is reckoned
Ample to assume it all:
Shadowy table, ceiling, wall,
England, Europe, Infinite Space,
Human History, Hell, and Grace.—
Proof of Mind's dominion, yes,
And remembrancer, no less,
Of its bondage. For the beauty
Is, one must report for duty
Whether 'minded' to, or no;
And, with five dull wits to show,
Answer for survival. So—
Adsum! Ici! Pronto! Sto!
Present and correct!
                                        But oh,
What a hubbub whistles in
Through that window! What a din
Electrifies the darkness! What
Rumour has the garden got—
Very Late Night Special—hot
News of something that was not
Dreamed, nor will be soon forgot:
Something glorious beyond all
Presentiment? What do they bawl
In the branches—Death's Recall?
Sudden Breach in Eden's Wall?
Cancellation of the Fall?
The panes reluctantly allow
Some vision's in the garden now.

The window, tentatively square,
Suggests that dawn is only there
By innuendo of blind air;
Or as a concept in the mind
Of tired darkness, undefined;
Or as the deep, vibrating chord
That Chaos knew, before the Word.

Yet that dark air is thickly scored
For brilliant jubilation: scratched,
Scribbled over, stippled, hatched,
Asteriskily affrighted,
Flourished, starred and twi-high-lighted,
By noise: by news: by nouns and notes
That spark and bubble in dark throats.
From orchard, meadow, marsh and clearing,
Flushed and dove-tailed into hearing,
Flashing, fading—reappearing—
Name them all you can't—though look who
Simplifies the task: a cuckoo
Out on orbit may be heard,
Threading dusk with one gold word,
Round as planets . . . Now, a wren
Lit by the sill . . . This blackbird, then,
Still haunted by his April theme . . .
And there the thrush, whose phrases seem
To flicker with his own sunbeam.

The thrush, enlightener of the dark,
The blackbird demonstrating Bach,
The wren exploding into praise,
The chaffinch blissful with one phrase,
The curlew bubbling from a cloud,

The robin thinking thoughts out-loud,
The swift amazed at his own speed,
The starling glorified in greed,
The storm-cock pinnacled for shouting,
The tawny owl at dawn of doubting,
The thrush illumining the world,
The robin noting buds are pearled,
The blackcap's nimble sweet contralto,
The blackbird's almost human alto,
The green woodpecker's jubilee laugh,
The jay's reply in withering chaff,
The sparrow's cheep, engaging toy,
The cuckoo's perfect word for joy,
The willow-warbler's plaintive scale,
The heart-ache of the nightingale,
The cuckoo's password to far summer,
The snipe's tattoo, the distant drummer,
The yellow-hammer's roadside greeting,
The nightingale's divine entreating,
The magpie's ill-appointed clatter,
The blackbird with a tune to scatter,
The whitethroat's tune in fiddle-snatches,
The blackbird's roundelazy catches,
The dunnock's commongrace of ditty,
The starlings' ways-and-means committee,
The ring-dove, rhythmic in the trance,
The robin's brief, observant glance,
The turtle-dove's patrician dolour,
The starling's loud defence of squalor,
The rook's dry comment and the crow's,
The one urbane, the one morose,
The wren in gusto absolute,
The goldcrest shriller, but minute,

The fleeting sorrow of pewits,
The total tattle of tom-tits,
The gossiping of farmyard fowls,
The heavy breathing of young owls,
The rooster's swank, the gander's honk,
The blackbird's hint of César Franck,
The kingfisher with one bright cry,
The thrush like all a brightening sky,
The greenfinch with a bagpipe squeeze,
The starling with his bronchial wheeze,
The rooks around the tent of dawning,
The swifts that smooth the enormous awning,
The larks that lift its rippling crown,
The cocks that peg the skylines down,
The wood-lark fluting, soft and ripe,
The garden-warbler's bubble-pipe,
The chiffchaff pleased with his own name,
The thrush, with easting heart aflame,
The blue tit's penny-peep and skirr,
The green hilarious woodpecker,
The corn-crake somnolently grating,
The spotted woodpecker vibrating,
The five horizons of the cocks,
The cuckoo's vows (unorthodox),
The meadow-pipit's fading trill,
The blackbird diatonic still—
And still the thrush, no spark abating,
But light itself illuminating:
The mottled cry, the vocal gleam,
The minim ray, the quavered beam;
Light orchestration of the small,
Illuminumerable all . . .

Yes, the pillow. Yes, more in—
But down and in—and next the chin.
Yes, the sheet a trifle slacker:
Close the port-holes on the fracas.
Yes, or very nearly yes:
Still some matter for distress:
Falling short of full success:
Lack of absolute finesse:
Eiderdown in some excess?
Well, no matter, more or less:
Too unspecified to guess:
Too generic to express:
Too habitual to assess:
Too remote, now, to redress:
(Too much bliss for true distress):
Better, far, to acquiesce,
Act of grace, to acquiesce,
Verb synonymous with bless,
Verb of quasi-saintliness,
Vocables of pure caress:
Acqui ripe as velvet esce,
Acqui sleek as silken dress,
Acqui crisp as watercress,
Aquatinted aquacress . . .
Aquatint or Aquitaine?
Aquaduct and aquaplane,
Equatorial equitation,
Equiangular equation,
Oxymoron oxyless,
Wake me at tu quoque, yes.

Yes, indeed. And as you slide
Into Sleep's odd countryside,

While a-carefree-gain you sink
Over Eider's downland brink,
While your notions, crossed with follies,
Romp and streak away like collies,
While your happy heart-beats tramp
Down from daybreak's British Camp,
And with measured foot-fall sally
Into Snore's primeval valley—
Clock may crow and bird may chime,
Sun may hoot and factory climb,
Tractor yodel, milkman drum,
Steeple yap and spaniel hum,
Boy rev up and Bentley shout . . .
They've heard your *fiat*: 'Count me out!'
Your wish is on the whitening sill:
'Don't disturb me!' Nothing will.

Little could, in your condition:
Short, that is, of nuclear fission.
Not in all these hours of sleep
Have you rambled down so deep,
Where the ferns of fiction blind
Ancient landslips of the mind.
There, should some remote unease
Touch you, like a spectral breeze,
Whispering—'Beside your bed
Something waits your lifted head:
Something welcome, something wet,
Something hot'—allay the fret!
Turn the doubt on which it plays
Into flowering paraphrase,
And by figurative ways
Deeper into dreams recoil . . .

Your early cup will never spoil.
Though yet unsipped, it takes no chill,
Though madly tipped, it cannot spill—
It hangs upon the dresser still!
And all's inertia that will be
Coactive for that cup of tea.
The saucer's deep among the crocks;
The match undisparate in the box;
The kettle haunts the fairy ring,
But, short of fairies, waits to sing.
As for the rest, you may suppose
These quite as uninvolved as those.
The gas, it may be, hardly stirs
In dawn's maroon gasometers;
The milk, perhaps, is in the cow;
The tea—who knows?—in junk or dhow;
The sugar's scarcely out of cane;
And even the water—even the plain
White water's in the whispering main!

Not soon the crisis, then. Not soon
Rewarded loss, and dubious boon.
Not soon will come ambivalent up,
Unwanted, welcome, wide, the cup.
Yet come it will.—And, peradventure,
It won't incur one glance of censure,
While rounding off the script of dream
With certain flourishes of steam.

The Choice

This is the moment. This!
While the hand lolls on the desk
On the brink of decision, free
To act, or refrain, in the stare
Of the questioning sun.—And the sun
Only means the appalling risk
Incurred by the freedom! See
How the straight-fingered sun
Points to the ink-pot's tip,
Till one fierce liquid star
Breeds on the silver lip.
The grains throng in that light
As a question throngs between lids.

And the wren and a dismal fly
In a web (voices off, very slight)
Unnerve—doodling a border
In the margin of concentration.

All is correct. Say nothing!
All, all is in order:
Hand, page, pen,
In some intended relation,
In some way deeply elect.
Bird utters. Fly repines.
Dust's multiplied. Star glances.
And this the confounding point
From where possibilities start.
Erect at the bald cross-roads
The painted-out finger-post shines.

From here great roads depart
In contrary ways; but where
Nothing divulges. Only,
On this election all rests.
All hope in the choosing.
All peace in a balance.
All meaning lies there.

The Guest

Build the pillows plump as mushrooms,
Folding down the elated sheet.
Look to all courtesies of the night-time:
Lemon to sip, petit beurre to eat.
Try the bedside lamp. Lay out
Towels large as a cloud and kind.
Bring to the dressing-table one rose—
And read the same thought in the mirror's mind.
For he is expected. Can joy do less,
When it may not spread carpets and fall at his feet?

Strip the pillows, fold the bedding,
Draw a dust-sheet over the bed.
Release to their holes around the house
The books that flocked to his midnight head.
Pick up scraps of a letter. Empty
A vase where pins and pennies confer.
Then slide the curtains: keep that sun
From whitening chintz and wall-paper.
For he is gone. Now if any good thing
Was left for the saying, it stays unsaid.

And all the day we were brimming with plans
To entertain him and keep him near;
And half the night were examining ways
To relish him better, eye and ear.
Was there ever a moment when anyone said,
'Relax. He is here!'?

For Instance

Waking in the summered light,
Taking summer all at once
From an open window's mere
Common sweetness, from a fly
As it scribbles in and out
Jazzy over bed and sill,

Waking where the summered sea,
Flaking blue across the town,
Needs your recognizing joy,
Pleads with little frowns of shadow,
Glancing at your window, for
Answers you alone can give,

Waking with a summered mind
Shaking summer out like cloths
Brilliant from a window—think:
Millions have responded so,
Seething millions, come and gone,
Breathing sweetness, like the fly.

Waking with the sense of time
Aching, O perceive how time
Can no more of summer show
Than it shows—how summer is,
How it absolutely is,
Now, this morning, and for you.

Masterpieces

Leaning from picture-gallery walls with immense
Meaning, or whirling us vertically up with only
Plaster to break our fall into populous clouds,
Masterpieces uncolour themselves in decay.

Taking proportion alone to ennoble the daylight
Breaking on stone, and all the while sensing the beetle
Fast in the beam, the improver bent to his plan,
Masterpieces live impotent as a child.

Swimming the cool of ink-dark cathedrals like roses
Brimming with sun-bright rain great windows wheel.
Vaster by far the rose of the flash of unmaking.
Masterpieces know nothing to nip this bud.

All glide to some close. Impasto cracks.
Small the dust, but it whispers. Bleak the mind
That dutifully entertains the elimination
Of beauty. Luckily, One does not see them thus.

For these are the rockets towering out of the past,
To please an eye which cannot for all his worlds
Taste pleasure too often. Nothing will ever
Waste, that has caught, however lightly, a glance.

Up they have flowed, will flow, to honour the long
Nuptials of the Bride and the vigilant Groom.
Tossed out of Dresden, Ravenna, Arles, Amsterdam,
    Rome:
Lost to regard, in a mere millennium gone.

And below: the little parabolas, flat trajectories,
Which glow to a plan so busy, which bounce and shine.
Perpetual dawn they seem, one blur of praise,
That yet is grained with million flights and dyings.

So here: at the window, lit for its brief
Career by a sparking touch of the sun—
A glass. The humble scene engraved
Might pass for breath. This, too, a squib.

Token of nothing but patience, and possibly
Broken before once narrowly scanned:
Even this, involved in the bright business
Of bliss, an oblation of joy, unique.

A Triptych for Denny, 1903–1915

I THE MEETING

When I was fearful and new,
And fumbled at white ceilings,
You came to my cot and we met
On the broad terms of your smile.

Mile apart though we were,
As baby and brother suppose,
Our hands reached up and down
The whole height of the cliff.

If you remember me at all,
I must be the child
Your laughter persuaded to laugh
When life said cry.

I? I remember nothing.
I loved you once. I have kept
That thought like a photograph frame
I sometimes invent you to fill.

Still you look over the bars,
Twirling the go-between toy,
But I have gone out to the world's
Other notions of fun.

One of us finished, exact,
Caught in the amber of death.
The other still altering on
Through the weathers of now.

How shall they ever meet now—
The boy who laughs for the child,
And the middle-aged man
Who sighs for the boy?

II THE NAME

The name that was a joy,
The name that was a way
Of colouring each day,
The name that flew so easy
Through all that married house,
A bird in the family morning
Heard in peace of the mind
Down the street, up the stair,
A name ordinary everywhere,
That soon went with a fellow,
But was the first swallow,
Naturally first,

Became a fairy glen
Peeped at with wonder,
Became rose and tender
As an evensong church,
A name to tip-toe in,
A name sometimes to draw
From a jewel-case, with awe;
Became a little sound so sad,
Heard in prayers by the bed,
Squinting through fists
At the round back of the day;
So sorry but so little,
That slight diminished third.

The same shall not be mute,
The same shall be heard
Whispered loud and sweet
Down all the flights of wonder,
Up the glittering morning street:
In the rooms of our well-being
The bird of two light syllables
Be heard in the new, the unknown song,
With one fellow and many,
Rhyming clear with any—
The name that long ago
Was got by heart in a by-road,
On a brief stair, in a special room,
And shall always be so:
Small and special and the same.

III THE SILENCE

And I to remember nothing!
Let me stare through memory
To where my earliest pictures,
With nothing for background, tease

These. Bright boughs, bright sunlight
Down a road: I purling along,
My stick in a glad clatter
Over palings. Beyond them, our home.

Moment of zest! Then a moment
Tumid with midnight: a room
Of illness: thick smell of some lamp
I must breathe in the night-light's glow.

Oh, but that was your night,
Illness, wonder, unrest!
I am looking right into your presence.
In the room one away you are there,

Sharing the counterfeit sunset,
The murmuring patterns. You meant
By 'Mother' the same quick yearning.
Odd that that should seem odd!

God called you, she said. So we let you
Drop into silence—left you
To the drowned rooms and the silence
Of the old home. In the new

Grew what I really remember.
The poker-knob tasted of brass.
The old dog smouldered by the bureau.
And the dining-room clock

Mocked my reading of timelessness,
When my father's preoccupied whistle
Curled on; or the afternoon sun
Dozed in some picture's brown cave.

Grave, boring, sweet,
The furnished world of a child!
And almost all of it wholly
Familiar to you, whom we never

Ever once mentioned. For years
You'd have accepted our rooms,
Even looks, without horror: simply
'We have moved house!' you'd have cried.

I'd your left-off world
To wear, your outgrown loves
To grow like you in. But these
Things hide what I pursue

Through and through them. The boy.
The face. The living truth
That went into nowhere too quick
For recollection to come.

Somewhere I cannot come,
That face, unmemoried, hides,
To be got once more by heart,
To be instantly recognized.

Who Cares?

Years ago, now, a man
Came to work in this garden
For the odd afternoon. A face
Pulled horizontal by some
Chronic self-justification—
Sense of a water-tight case
Against (if it ever were heard)
Everything. When he volunteered, 'I'm
Not afraid of hard work!',
I no longer expected it of him,
Perceiving he meant in the sense
He did not fear polio or piles.
One Autumn he came for: then stopped.
No words, no unpleasantness!
He went of his own flat will.
I never liked the fellow.

This morning in church, the brief
Interpolated sentence, breaking
The well-rubbed verbal perspective.
'Pray for the soul of——' of him
I mean. 'May he rest in peace!'
Phrase like a pulse of current
Through my kneeling heart, off guard.
Oh, is he dead, then? A view
Of the sour-puss grin by the tank,
Of the back complacent with braces
(Like the obverse), going down paths—
Going all down one Autumn
With a load of inhibited grudge,

And nothing good ever done
Between us. No true greeting.
I never cared for the type.

Ah, the heart has its moments, surely;
Touches grace in remorse!
And regret is better than nothing:
Might even pass for a meeting
In retrospect, as between
Two ghosts. . . . All said and done,
He was here three months, to be exact.
Not like a life-time's companion,
A well-loved servant. No friend.
And his attitude, to be candid,
Was obstructive. It palpably does
Take two for a friendship. And he'd
No mind to be friendly—and no
Satisfaction in the job. Oh, he lacked
All sense of the dignity of labour!
Who does care for that type?

A Bridge on the Usk

An hour has passed and we are standing yet,
Four elbows on the zig-zag parapet,
In one saw-tooth
Of an old bridge built out to cleave the weight
Of calculated winters in full spate,
But at this season,
When heat has put the clear October glaze
On self-illuminated leaves that praise
The Apostle named,
Feeling no greater push than bridges know
From warm down-water wind and luke-warm flow;
So the high arches
Drink mouthfuls of air mostly and resound
With a loud, shallow, summer-emptying sound;
And so, an hour,
Between them we have watched the silver smother
Move the green fingers one way and the other,
And held in gaze
The onward hands dividing and dividing,
Deep in the huge hypnosis of that gliding.

At first when we
Came with our troubles, paused and looked amazed
Along a river vista where it blazed
Out of a mountain
That fell unfalling with a clear blue note
Thin as the sky and hardly less remote,
It seemed each sharp
Particular stroke of evening shine—the dark
Scribble of a swallow—quick exclamation-mark

Of fish that flopped
Back into brief geometry—the intense
Disquiet in a balloon of gnats—the sense
That every tree
On either bank perspectively before us
Added and knew it added to a chorus
Of luminous limbs—
And when the staring eyes were long attached
To the swift current, presently they watched
Out of each corner
The loosened scenery begin edging back—
All seemed to be imbued with our own lack
Of inward peace,
That gift which crowds the summer in the comb
And reckons Anywhere a name for home;
Which being missed
The senses' garden lies in disarray,
And cold, however warm, and very far away:
Or else, or else
The harmony was there and surely real,
But only mocked us that we could not feel
Our place in it,
Because though beautiful in the extreme
This beauty was like someone else's dream.

Now all is subtly altered by the mere
Act of not acting, pausing, leaning here,
Thinking no words,
Unless the occasional murmur lips may form
For silence to stay meaningful, and warm;
Letting the river
Wash out complexity from life, as tears
Wash grit away until the eyesight clears

Bright with relief;
So that we see in all these forms which fall
To their simplicities of dusk a parable
Of our own state,
Or rather see the fabric of the mind
Drawn out into the view and redesigned
At cool remove—
Observing patiently before our faces
The jig-saw pieces drawn to their right places,
The problem solved.

Now the tree'd margins illustrate for us
How rich is simple and how luminous
A living black;
The mountains modulate to walls of grey,
Their background of gold-leaf all rubbed away
By fingering thought;
Dark lights in the white mirror oscillate;
Light answering darks, which may be bats, vibrate;
Yet both contrive
To seem the very pulse of calm, and thicken
The quality of stillness which they quicken;
And all grows plain
In some few tones that bless a distant hill
That blesses a known valley that must still
Live in that glow;
In some few colours that externalize
The found solution of a life that lies
Before us now,
Like the stream's page of uncorrupted white
On which the imagination leans to write;
And write it will.

And still it slides
Meanings to take—a multiple soft roar

Heightened with white, a moving vocal floor,
A printless sheet,
Out of each lovelier moment of less light
Into the press and proffer of new night;
Out of those hills
Where a great light once lived, translating it,
Into obscurity, to serve and fit
Our humbler need;
Out of a large kind light into a dusk,
Still full of poetry and still procreant, Usk
Roars rich as thought.

Notes

FORE-RHYME

I give this name to a method whereby the rhyme falls on the first beat of the line instead of, conventionally, on the last. Though clearly no rival to orthodox rhyming, it may evoke, on occasion, a certain feeling of freshness, and 'attack'. I hope it contributes to the sense of anticipation in 'The Unlit Passage' (p. 86), where, in a place of memories, a wished-for figure is imagined as approaching, only to vanish, again and again, as if played back in a film.

In end-rhyming the rhyme must sound on the last syllable or syllables of complete words. To rhyme 'fast' with 'masterpiece' (carrying the final syllables over into the following line), could only be comic. Not so in fore-rhyme. There we may rhyme on syllables followed as well as preceded by others unrhyming: 'halting' with 'falters', 'divinely' with 'resign'; also 'fret' with 'sets', which in end-rhyming is always slovenly.

Similarly in double rhymes we may rhyme not only 'damply' with 'amplitude' but 'survival' with 'rivalry'. The only rule is that the rhyme must fall on the first stressed syllable. Thus 'slow in the ...' can rhyme with 'although'. But if the stress is divided there may be a choice. To 'odd, though, how actual ...' the rhyme could be 'God' or 'flow'. Other fore-rhymed poems are 'Jay's Feather' (p. 35), 'This Wood for Context' (p. 60), 'For Instance' (p. 108), and 'Masterpieces' (p. 109).

A WOVEN SONNET

A new form in which the rhymes are so woven that each is completed at three lines' remove, except that the sonnet begins and ends with a closer pair for emphasis:

a–b–a–c–b–d–c–e–d–f–e–g–f–g.

Unequal division into octave and sestet is one of the beauties of the sonnet, though not obligatory. It does not need to be reflected in the rhyme-scheme. Petrarch's pattern presupposes it; Shakespeare's and Drayton's hardly point to it; Spenser's not at all. The suggested form is with Spenser's in this: the division, if marked, will be marked in the content alone. Milton followed Petrarch (and Wordsworth Milton) in dividing the pattern – but overran or completely effaced a corresponding division in the sense. Here the reverse is generally proposed: the sense divided – the pattern running on. Alternatively, by the transposition of two sounds, first e and second d, the woven sonnet can be broken, with octave and sestet formed on the same principal, but separately. Experiments in the woven form are sonnets on pp. 67, 69, 71, 72, 79, 85, 90, and in the broken-woven those on pp. 36, 80, 83, 91, 94. The last is in one-syllable words.

'Under the Breath', p. 51. In the form of linked Haikus: seventeen syllables distributed between three lines.

'Reveries Around Eurydice', p. 54. The allusion in II is to the version of the myth in Gluck's opera, where Eurydice, not understanding, entreats Orpheus to turn.

'Laughter All Round', p. 85. In Signorelli's fresco in Orvieto Cathedral the resurrected greet their own laughing skeletons.

'A Bridge on the Usk', p. 118. In the last stanzas there are allusions to Vaughan, who lived upstream from the bridge, and to his poem on the Usk, 'To the River Isca'.

Afterword

BY CHRISTOPHER BOOKER

In the autumn of 1934, a young man just down from Oxford wrote a sonnet for a friend, the daughter of Sir Edwin Lutyens, who lived in an ancient house in Northumberland. The poem was intended as a 'charm' to bring the house good fortune, and something inspired its author to scratch his sonnet on a windowpane. Obtaining from somewhere a diamond-tipped pencil, he wrote out the sonnet in beautiful calligraphy, decorated it at the end with the image of an urn full of wild flowers, and the window was installed in 1935.

Little did Laurence Whistler realise how that moment of inspiration was to change his life. At the time he had no thought for the future other than that he would be a poet, a conviction which seemed to be confirmed a few months later when, as an unknown twenty-three-year-old, he was chosen to be the first winner of the King's Gold Medal for Poetry. It was true he had also already shown talent as a visual artist, as in the addition of the urn as a tailpiece to his first glass engraving – but in this respect he felt completely overshadowed by his elder brother Rex Whistler, who was already winning a brilliant reputation for his book illustrations, stage sets and murals.

Nevertheless fate had cast its die. Unwittingly, by those first scratchings with a diamond point on glass, Laurence Whistler had already taken his first step towards recreating an art form which had virtually been dead for a hundred and fifty years, and towards the career which for decades now has established him as this country's leading artist in engraved glass. His precise, luminous pictures, picked out in light from the darkness of the glass, are unlike any other works of art created in our time. They are treasured in private collections all over Britain, and can be seen in chapels and churches ranging from Moreton in Dorset (where Whistler has engraved every one of the twelve large windows) to Sherborne Abbey and Salisbury Cathedral.

Whistler has also won a considerable reputation as a writer of prose, notably with his books about the two people closest to his inner life. The Initials in the Heart, *published in 1964 and reissued several times since, most recently in 1987, has made a profound impression on countless readers with its moving account of his life with his first wife Jill Furse, a wonderfully beautiful actress and rare spirit, who died only five years after their marriage, in October 1944. In 1985 he published* The Laughter and the Urn, *a life of his brother Rex, who was killed on service as a tank commander in Normandy in the summer of the same year, 1944.*

What is less well-known about Laurence Whistler is the extent to which, at different times over the past fifty years, he has continued to pursue his original vocation as a poet. Nevertheless no one who knows Whistler's glass engravings or his prose writing well could be surprised to discover that he is also a poet. So many of his engravings are like visual poems – with their use of observed details of nature to symbolise the inner landscape of human experience, their meditations on the rhythms of winter and spring, death and life, darkness and light. Equally his prose writing always has a poetic feel about it, in its conjuring up of mood and detail, its sense of the deeper significance of the passing moment in nature or in a relationship between two people – Lord David Cecil described The Initials in the Heart *as 'one of the most sustainedly beautiful (prose) poems I have read for a long time'.*

The poems which open this selection by Laurence Whistler from his life's work are taken from Who Live in Unity. *They were written in an army camp in Yorkshire in 1944 (indeed they were first printed and published in the same camp, by his wife's cousin) and they are all directly inspired by his love for Jill, then living with their small son Simon in Devon. Like all good love poems, they elevate a particular love into something timeless and universal. They are filled with awe at how deeply such a love for another can evoke a sense of eternity, of a complete unity and perfection. In the lines*

The total rose—
Now surely love is finite in that rose!

Whistler uses an image which was to return in his work in a totally different context forty years later, in two of the finest of his glass engravings, a pair of commemorative panels in Salisbury Cathedral, in which the 'rose of fulfilment' shining with the perfect light of eternity floats above a dream-like downland landscape. In one poem the verse endings taken from the liturgy, 'No secrets are hid', 'Take, eat', 'And remain with you always', mingle the sacredness of earthly love with the holiest of all loves, showing how one is a particular aspect of the other. In another poem the verse ending 'This is the house that God built' is refined through 'This is the house' to the final bare statement 'This is', like a Zen affirmation of all that can or need be said about the universe.

Then the mood changes. The scarcely believing joy of the poems written to a loved wife in the first part of 1944 was suddenly, devastatingly cut short by Jill's fatal illness in the autumn of that year, just after she had given birth to their second child. On her deathbed Laurence was able to give her a copy of the poems he had written to her, but she was too weak to read them in print and could only hold them in her hands, and for a long time afterwards the desire to write poetry left him.

Some years later it began to creep back, only now his inspiration was to recreate those days with Jill in the new world without her.

As we lay thinking side by side,
One afternoon years back . . .
It seemed to me a shadow-man
Hung in the door to watch.

The 'shadow-man' was the writer's own ghost, imagined as returning long after her death. But she could still conjure up in him that sense of eternity so powerful that it demanded to be put into poetry. Over many years he continued to write poems full of remembered details of their brief life together – the jay's feather thrown into a stream – lying in bed in a darkened room lit only by the glow of an electric fire. Eventually this sequence of poems seemed ready for publication, under the title To Celebrate her Living, *and it appeared in 1967 as a companion volume to* The Initials in the Heart, *published three years before.*

The poems which end the present selection begin with some on other themes, originally published in the years when To Celebrate her Living *was still taking shape. The triptych for Denny, from* Audible Silence *(1961), commemorates a third great loss of Laurence's life, the death in childhood of a third brother (of which he has written in the early chapters of* The Laughter and the Urn*). 'A Sedative At Daybreak', one of a selection from* The View from this Window *(1956), strikes a rather different note from everything else in this collection, with its entertaining catalogue of characterisations of birdsong.*

Finally, later than the rest, comes 'A Bridge on the Usk' (1976), which turns a long rest on a Welsh bridge, looking down into the dark, swirling waters and out to the mountains beyond, into a meditation on the healing power of such a rest to calm jangled thoughts and feelings into a state of stillness,

> The jig-saw pieces drawn to their right places,
> The problem solved

and this culminates in an evocation of the great mystical poet of light Henry Vaughan, who lived a few miles away, up-stream.

As so often in Whistler's work, the imagery which runs through the poem is of darkness dissolving into light. But behind this, as behind all the poems in this book, lies the still deeper sense which Whistler crystallised in the introduction to his latest book of engravings, Scenes and Signs on Glass, *when he wrote 'the light* needs *the dark to become articulate'. On one level, this has been the nature of the process whereby, with his diamond tip, he has conjured living images of extraordinary power out of the darkness of a piece of glass. On another it has been the story of his life and of how, both for himself and for others, he has shown that only through the darkness of loss, uncertainty and disarray is it finally possible to come to a sense of the true light which exists beyond time and for ever.*